We native English speakers have long had a talent for mucking up our own language. Mastering proper English, even for the most educated Anglo, is no easy task. So, it comes as little surprise that those non-native English speakers who aren't as tuned in to the subtleties of English get things delightfully twisted despite their best efforts to cater to us by putting up signs. You have to give them credit for trying, though. Who among us would have the courage to put up a sign in a foreign language? Just imagine the hilarity if we tried to cover our English-speaking lands with signs for Russian, Turkish, or Chinese tourists. We'd walk around completely unaware of gaffes that would have these travelers rolling with laughter in our streets. Do you think we'd take the time to crosscheck spellings, grammar and possible double entendres in even a small percentage of the world's roughly 6,800 known languages (2,261 of which have writing systems)? I wouldn't be too surprised if the word "signspotting" translates to something bizarre in another tongue (I've never bothered to check). With some luck, the name will end up creating a lingual stir of its own in at least one language.

Many gaffes on signs around the world have been written down and shared. You many have seen some of these in a newspaper article, book or chain email. The classics include a menu claiming "the waiter passes all water" or a hotel sign stating "all guests will be serviced by the chamber maid." The trouble with these now legendary signs is that, despite much searching, I wasn't able to find photos of them. After some time, I was forced to conclude that many of them come from the same place jokes are hatched: someone's fertile imagination.

Funny signs have appeared in proof-positive photo form in various publications and on various websites for years. The images in this book represent the best of the collection I have been amassing for the last ten years (five years privately, five publicly). Since 2000, people have been sending their favorite shots to my website, and the ones selected have been published in various North American newspapers. Thanks to the Lonely Planet email newsletter, *Comet,* more and more funny signs are now sent in by travelers from around the world. Those people whose photos were picked for publication received US$50, and a few lucky signspotters have collected a Star Alliance round-the-world ticket for their submissions. To check out the current annual grand prize or to submit a photo you'd like to share, please visit www.signspotting.com.

# THE AUTHOR

Doug Lansky spent ten years backpacking the planet, during which time he visited 120 countries (if you count San Marino). He has written a syndicated newspaper travel column, penned several books, and hosted a Discovery Channel show. Doug started collecting photos of funny signs during the first year of his travels, and it has turned into a disturbingly addictive habit.

THIS LIGHT
NEVER TURNS
GREEN

LOCATION: FORT WALTON BEACH, FLORIDA, USA   CREDIT: RICHARD GAEBLER

Welcome to the traffic light from hell. At least it lets you know where you stand…or sit, idling in park, forever.

こまちのりばは後方（盛岡側）へ

For Akita Shinkansen Komachi,
Go back toward your behind.

There's a Japanese proverb that says, "The reverse side also has a reverse side."
It seems that in this case they've tried to employ it literally.

LOCATION: LOS ANGELES, CALIFORNIA, USA   CREDIT: JUDY CARR

Once they get on the freeway, it's OK.

PROMISED LAND
CLOSED
LE  /4 MILE

All traffic will be temporarily rerouted through Mecca.

It's pronounced just as it looks.

Cruise Ships
USE
AIRPORT EXIT

LOCATION: SAN DIEGO, CALIFORNIA, USA   CREDIT: ROBERT VAIS

It's nice to see the travel industry consolidating.

Hey kids, forget the amusement park – it's open-house fun day at the funeral home!
Last one in the car is a rotting corpse.

灌木林步行徑

若非與經驗步行者同行，
請勿步過警告牌。

등산길 경고문

등산에 관한 전문지식이나 경험이 작으신
분들은 이 표지판 뒤로 넘어가지말아주시길
바랍니다.

ブッシュ・ウォーキング(山歩き)
コース

ブッシュ・ウォーキング(山歩き)の熟練者
以外は、これより先には行かないで
下さい。

THIS SIGN IS TO PREVENT FOREIGN
TOURISTS FROM GETTING LOST

Finally, helpful tourist information.

Well, you can't blame them for calling it as they
see it.

Perhaps only in Michigan, America's automotive heartland, do people need to be reminded that pedestrians may actually be on foot.

LOCATION: PICTURED ROCKS NATIONAL LAKESHORE, MICHIGAN, USA
CREDIT: SHIRLEY REEVE

Do you suppose this would include the annual trip to visit the in-laws?

LOCATION: MOLINE, ILLINOIS, USA
CREDIT: JEAN OLMSTEAD

How exactly one should prepare for an unseen burst of live ammunition is perplexing, since it's not – due to nitpicky legal minutiae – included in most driving examinations.

LOCATION: DORSET, ENGLAND
CREDIT: CHARLES FREAN

Are the San Juan Islands the recreational vehicle side-view mirror smack-down capital of the world, or just the only place that warns you about them?

Here's an interesting reflection on Western society: we even have parking spots for people who have just made a conscious decision not to park.

Forget cloning and high-tech laboratories – a team of contractors will do.

LOCATION: DECEPTION PASS, SAN JUAN ISLANDS, WASHINGTON, USA
CREDIT: BART ZIEGLER

LOCATION: BURLEIGH, WISCONSIN, USA
CREDIT: WILLIAM KUCHARSKI

LOCATION: MOZAMBIQUE, NEAR THE MALAWI BORDER
CREDIT: IAN MCCART

# TRAFFIC FLAWS

When you visit a new country, you're not allowed to vote. You can't cash a personal check. Your library card isn't valid. Yet they let you drive. They let you get behind the wheel of a multi-ton vehicle and zip around anywhere you please. Most countries don't even ask you to have an International Driver's License; for those that do, there's no need to sit a test to get one. Roughly US$10 and a valid driver's license presented at any major auto club in your home country will suffice. Never mind that in some European countries it takes US$1500 and nine months of driver-training classes to get a license. Somehow foreigners are expected to navigate the road and pick up the traffic nuances – perhaps even adjust to a steering wheel on the opposite side of the car while driving on the opposite side of the road – before making their first lane change.

If that isn't demanding enough, there are the signs to contend with. And these are not confined to the symbols that look like psych-test ink blots. There are also signs that look woefully out of place (why do we need to know about an approaching wind sock?). And it's hard to forget the occasional screwball posting that almost stops us in our tracks – if we could just locate the brakes fast enough in that rental car! Fortunately for us, a few daring drivers were able to find a place to pull over, get out and snap a picture. It's not always that easy. Some signs whiz by at warp speed, and it's too difficult to negotiate your way back through the traffic to take a photograph.

If you're lucky enough to decipher the meaning of the many perplexing road signs, the next challenge is to work out which ones are the most important. In many countries, few traffic laws are followed to the letter. When I heard that Napoli, Italy, had the world's worst drivers, I headed that way to rent a car – just for kicks. The biggest challenge was working out which laws the locals were ignoring. Traffic lights, for example, carried about as much significance as the lights on a Christmas tree. People stopped for them, but only if they felt like it. Drivers seemed to follow a Darwinian philosophy: right of way belonged to the driver who looked most determined not to stop.

Here's one theory: maybe "Three Mile Village" was already taken.

LOCATION: KANAB, UTAH, USA   CREDIT: CAROLE MCLAUGHLIN

**ALL INTERNATIONAL PASSENGERS WITH LUGGAGE INCLUDING CANADA MUST BE CHECKED IN AT TICKET COUNTER BY AGENT**

Would today's X-ray security equipment be able to detect Canada?

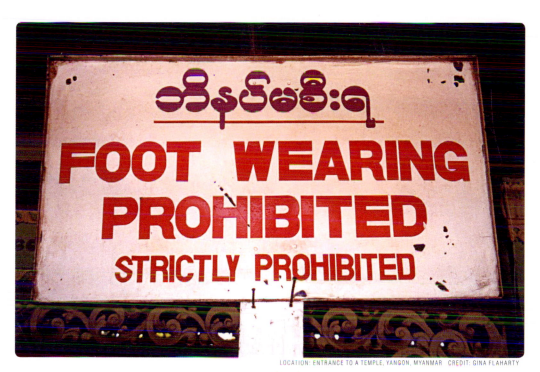

It's hard to blame them. Have you smelled travelers' feet lately?

ZONA ARQUEOLÓGICA DE
MONTE ALBÁN
OAXACA

**¡Cuidado! El agua de los baños no es para beber y por favor...**

**¡No la desperdicie!**

**Warning! Water for the toilet is not drinkable**

Well, gee, normally drinking out of the toilet in Mexico is just fine.
Hard to imagine what the problem might be in this instance.

When life imitates a *Far Side* cartoon.

LOCATION: AUBURN, CALIFORNIA, USA   CREDIT: ROGER PERKINS

Press release:
Reno to be reached by right turns only.

LOCATION: SHAWANO, WISCONSIN, USA   CREDIT: FAITH HAMMOND

New and improved humans.

**Toad Suck Park**
**NEXT RIGHT**

LOCATION: NEAR LITTLE ROCK, ARKANSAS, USA  CREDIT: MURRAY LEIBOWITZ

According to local legend, this park (yes, it is an actual park) was a popular spot for bargemen to drink rum. They are said to have "sucked on bottles until they swelled up like toads." Now there's an image worthy of commemoration.

If you can read this, either you're driving too high or flying too low.

Welcome to the Red Light District of the animal kingdom.

Aren't the Jamaican police great? They can stop crime with their eyes closed.

LOCATION: MAUI, HAWAII, USA
CREDIT: ROBERT HAWLEY

LOCATION: LIVERPOOL, ENGLAND
CREDIT: JOANNE WINGE

LOCATION: DUNN RIVER FALLS PARK, JAMAICA
CREDIT: MICHAEL KERRICK

A dump for a Trump.

It looks as though the Swedes have discovered the key to slowing down speeding men: speed bumps with cleavage.

Two wrongs don't make a right, but three rights make a left. This is evidently what happens when they let civil engineers graduate early.

LOCATION: CHELSEA HEIGHTS, NEW JERSEY, USA
CREDIT: YOLANDA NAGY

LOCATION: STOCKHOLM, SWEDEN
CREDIT: DOUG LANSKY

LOCATION: DANVILLE, ILLINOIS, USA
CREDIT: SKOT LATONA

STREET
DEPT
PROPERTY

THIS IS
NOT A
STREET

City of Lake Geneva
STREET DEPARTMENT

LOCATION: LAKE GENEVA, WISCONSIN, USA  CREDIT: MIKE FRANZENE

We know a street when we see one.

PARADISE 12 km
NO EXIT

GREENSTONE 29 km

ROUTEBURN 18 km

KINLOCH 18 km

PRIORY RD
NO EXIT

Paradise found: only 12km, mind the "no exit" warning.

"Hi. I'm looking for representation. I just drove into a sign and hurt my neck."

TOILET
▶

STAY IN
YOUR CAR

OZONJUITI M'BARI
19 KM ▶

OKAUKUEJO
◀ 41 KM

Now here's a challenge for even the most experienced traveler. With wild animals roaming this Namibian game park, you may not have much choice but to hone your target practice.

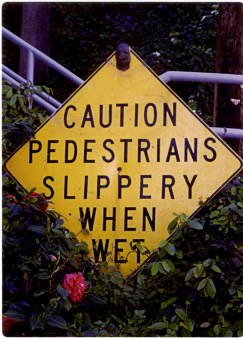

Just add a little water and those Bay Area pedestrians start slipping right out of your hands.

Is there any good way to promote this cleaning product? How about: "Use Barf, and you'll get noticed." Or maybe: "Wow, Mom, you smell like Barf!"

Ah, but of clouse.

So that's where they make horses.

# FAILED MARKETING

Large corporations spend hundreds of millions of dollars on marketing. Yet when they begin to introduce their successful products to other cultures, they often run into linguistic landmines. This has been well documented, and Web servers around the globe are filled with these gaffes. Some of the most famous incidents are pure urban legend, such as the case of the Ford Motor Company introducing their successful car, the Pinto, to Brazil. In Portuguese "pinto" is slang for male genitalia ("Hey guys, guess what? I've got a new Pinto!"). In fact, the car wasn't sold in Brazil, though a handful may have been imported. However, the name was changed to Corcel (meaning "horse") well in advance of sales. Nevertheless, "I've got my horse parked outside" may cause another sort of confusion.

Not all such stories are myth. For example, Pepsi's slogan "Come Alive with the Pepsi Generation" was launched in Taiwan and directly translated as "Pepsi brings your ancestors back from the dead."

The KFC slogan "Finger-Lickin' Good" was translated into Chinese as "Eat Your Fingers Off!" Even in a country where some people eat dogs, snake blood, scorpions and grasshoppers, this was unappetizing.

While we shouldn't feel guilty for enjoying the humor that comes from non-English speakers grappling with another language, we should at least be able to sympathize – many examples in this book illustrate that native English speakers often find the nuances of their own language just as challenging!

KASHGA[

Westen & Chinese foo

welcome big

南北大菜 内设

"Big nose" is slang for Westerner – it sounds insensitive, but it's not meant to insult.
And besides, it's better than being their "plastic surgery friends."

# CAFE

## English menu

*se friends*

6, 8, 10元小學

Apparently they're now putting seats in the drive thru.
Doesn't this rather defeat the purpose of staying in your car?

The minibar of this hotel is stocked with a full selection of antihistamines.

Yes, there's a free demo included with each visit to this rest room.

LOCATION: SAN DIEGO, CALIFORNIA, USA   CREDIT: WILLIAM BROWN

Hey, it's Southern California. You don't break a sweat until you have to.

LOCATION: LAKE DISTRICT, ENGLAND   CREDIT: NANCY HOEY

Welcome to Heave Hotel. The B&B&B concept has obviously paid off – the hotel is full.

PIQUE NIQUE
PIC NIC AREA
PICK NICK PLATZ
AREA DE PIC NIC
AREA PER EL PIC NIC

LOCATION: CHÂTEAU DE CHENONCEAU, FRANCE   CREDIT: KATIE MILLER

It looks like a team of translators was brought in for this task. Or maybe it was just one guy making them up. In which case, he forgot "el picko nicko" and "piazza del pica nica."

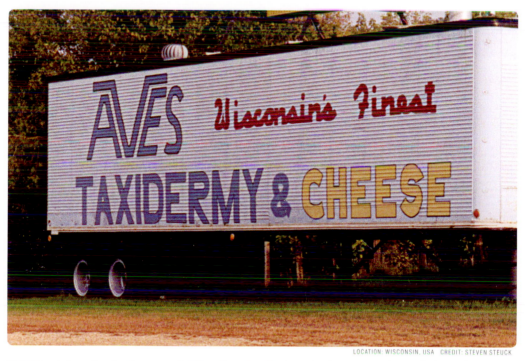

Here's an interesting business model: lure them in with the animal mounting, then sell them cheese. Presumably, the cheese is incredibly lifelike.

LOCATION: TAIPEI, TAIWAN   CREDIT: MARILYN TANK

We've had dry ice and dry-cleaning for a while now. This was just a matter of time.

TORTURE CHAMBER
UNSUITABLE FOR
WHEELCHAIR USERS

LOCATION: WARWICK CASTLE, ENGLAND   CREDIT: HOLLIS TISCHNER

What happened to equal-opportunity pain inflictors? Sue the bastards.

Don't worry, it's only Sasquatch.

Outside of Wisconsin Rapids, this is simply known as "parking." I'm not sure how it works when the "drive-up" option isn't offered.

התתשלום מראש בקופה

**PAYMENT BEFORE ORDERING**

LOCATION: BEN GURION AIRPORT, ISRAEL   CREDIT: ROBERT HOFMANN

Pay first, choose later.

↑ **Chigwell**
**Stanford Rivers** A 113

← **Brentwood**
**Kelvedon Hatch** A 128
**Industrial Estates**

Secret Nuclear Bunker

Pssst. Can you keep a secret?

LOCATION: MILL VALLEY, CALIFORNIA, USA   CREDIT: PETER YOUNG

Now here's a recipe for disaster.

LOCATION: MINGORA, PAKISTAN   CREDIT: GEORGE TOLLES

Would we get more publicity if we trimmed that marijuana patch so people could see our sign?

Now if it was worms and orange juice, that would be another story.

Hey, blind people, look here!

Tourists have probably been wondering what all that yellowish grainy stuff is that they've been driving through for hours.

Please drive carefully.
Our children are extremely slow.

Buy the house now and we'll throw in the owner for free. He's good company, handy with a vacuum, and doesn't play country-and-western music after 9pm.

# ACCIDENTAL PORN

Pornography is many things, but rarely does it get called an accident. This is, of course, our word for it. The people putting up pornlike signs probably never knew (and still don't) of any sexual innuendo. I'm sure most of them, including the residents of Pussy, France, wouldn't take evasive action anyway. Many of these signs, as porn aficionados would surely point out, are not actually pornographic in nature at all, but just a word or innuendo typically reserved for cable TV. To the traveler looking for guidance on the road, though, that's close enough.

There will be no in-depth examination here about why inadvertent sexual connotations are deliciously funny. Or about how exactly they conjure up that slightly guilty, naughty laugh. Put simply, these signs have the ability to strike us in that vulnerable humor spot right where low-brow bottoms out. At least I imagine that's why travelers send in so many of these kind of images.

In theory, they should take away only your money here.
And the only thing that is inflated is the exchange rate.

LOCATION: CANCUN, MEXICO   CREDIT: JAMI NHOLSONIC

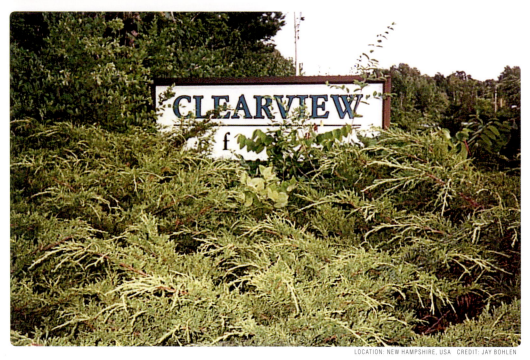

It's hard to read the text beneath "Clearview." Maybe it says "of this bush" or "in the other direction."

We like to think we're better than your average erection company.

LOCATION: CHAPEL HILL, NORTH CAROLINA, USA   CREDIT: JAMES FOLKER

Pennies for heaven.

Stöckelschuhe verboten!
High-heeled shoes

Ankles away!

Well, the parishioners have been duly warned.

Try our gastrointestinal daily specialty.

◀ 獸 籠

# WILD MAMMA LS EXHIBITS

On the bright side, if the sign were just a little wider it would have read, "wild mammal sex hibits."

Who said all roads lead to Rome? Welcome to Windjammer (neighborhood motto: Windjammer!)

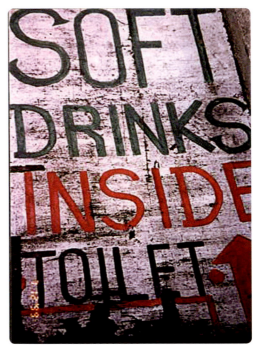

At least they're cold.

LOCATION: REDWOOD NATIONAL PARK, CALIFORNIA, USA   CREDIT: SKOT LATONA

Where I come from we just call that sand.
Or desert.

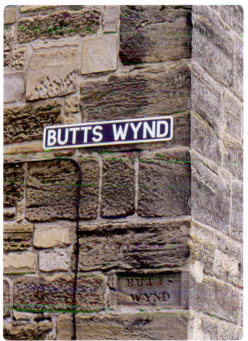

LOCATION: ST ANDREWS, SCOTLAND  CREDIT: DOUG LANSKY

Finally, an explanation for the unusually stiff
breezes that frequent this golfing mecca.

Prophecy: "I predict you will save thirty percent on a pair of used jeans."

LOCATION: MITCHELL, SOUTH DAKOTA, USA  CREDIT: WILLIAM CUMMING

There's nothing like a few hunters roaming the premises to help drum up some business. Maybe they should change the name of the hospital to "Almost Safe Haven."

RELAX

SLIDE AREA ENDS

LOCATION: KARAKORUM HIGHWAY, PAKISTAN   CREDIT: DALE SIEVERT

Some roads have scenic overlooks. The rough, high-altitude Karakorum Highway between Pakistan and China has relaxation areas.

Here's the good news: the cuisine couldn't possibly taste worse than it sounds.

"Welcome to Ethel" might have been more appropriate.

Here's something you wouldn't expect to see: flora on the move.

It sounds like a new recipe for scrambled eggs. And indigestion.

With practical reminders like these, drivers can have their valuables ready for quick handover.

# EXPERIENTIAL TRAVEL

Anyone who has spent time traveling in less developed parts of the world, such as…well, Italy, has probably come across a squat toilet. Some travelers embrace the new experience, but many simply venture in, take a cursory look at the hole in the floor, and then decide they can wait.

In other words, the act of going to the toilet, thinking about going but deciding not to, or even holding it in for the duration of your trip is a topic of much conversation. Typically, such talk is between friends; magazines and newspapers tend to steer clear of the topic for fear they may set off low-brow alarms. Yet when this conversation does make it into the media it elicits a huge response. I wrote a nationally syndicated newspaper travel column for five years, and it was my one article on toilets of the world that received the largest reader response for a single story: more than 200 letters and emails. What did my readers write? Their own personal toilet stories. One woman got her bum stuck in the loo; a man flooded a rustic-model toilet plus the restaurant it was located in; and one woman couldn't for the life of her figure out how to use the toilet and had to invite the café owner into the stall for clarification. All in all, it read like travel-toilet therapy. People had evidently been traumatized and were anxious to share their tales. Some had had it bottled up inside them for years – the story, that is!

People know that visiting a toilet in a foreign place can be traumatic. So what do locals do to ease anxiety? They put up signs. Which, sometimes, just makes matters worse.

It's really no surprise that rest-room-related signs are among the most frequently submitted.

LOCATION: ACADIA NATIONAL PARK, MAINE, USA   CREDIT: BARBARA KREGG

Nature is calling.

Sometimes it's easy to forget that people might be just as baffled by our toilets as we are by theirs.
I have yet to see a sign in a squat toilet instructing people not to sit directly on the hole in the floor, though.

Like, oh my god, let's totally live here.

LOCATION: CONIFER, COLORADO, USA  CREDIT: ANNE GRESS

LOCATION: EL MIRAGE FLATS, CALIFORNIA, USA   CREDIT: DOUG LANSKY

Ironically, if you just drive another few meters, you're on the famous unlimited-speed driving course.

I'm not quite sure what to make of this.

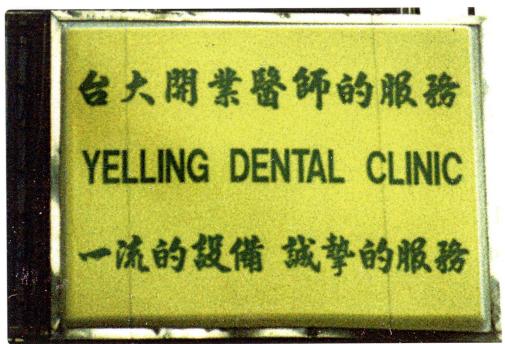

台大開業醫師的服務
YELLING DENTAL CLINIC
一流的設備 誠摯的服務

Maybe they could be more liberal with the painkiller.

Parking Pac-Man.

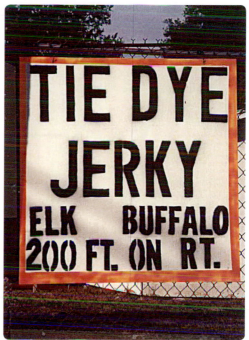

Which is more bizarre: the highly specific product selection of beef jerky and tie-dye or combining the two into one unappetizing (but colorful) snack?

Apparently, there's no fine for flagrant grammatical violations.

Did you ever wonder what life would be like if they let lawyers write street signs?

Giant tissue, anyone?

LOCATION: BADALING, CHINA
CREDIT: ROSANN MCCULLOUGH

LOCATION: FLORIDA, USA
CREDIT: MICHELLE PRETTITORE

LOCATION: PIGEON FORGE, TENNESSEE, USA
CREDIT: JERI PHILLIPS

Apparently, the former slogan
("Old Tires We Just Got!") wasn't
working so well.

Should you look both ways or just
duck?

New Orleans has evidently
instituted some strict new laws for
Mardi Gras.

LOCATION: PITTSBURGH, PENNSYLVANIA, USA
CREDIT: JESSICA WILLE

LOCATION: BIGLERVILLE, PENNSYLVANIA, USA
CREDIT: LISA BRAUGHLER

LOCATION: NEW ORLEANS, LOUISIANA, USA
CREDIT: RICHARD BRADFORD

श्री ५ को सरकार द्वारा स्विकृत

२.न.१८४५८/८००-०४८

सुपर पर्फेक्ट टाइप राइटिङ इष्टिच्यूट

# SUPER PERFCT TYPE WRITING INSTITUTE

यहाँ आधुनिक तरीकाले कम्प्युटरको लागि टाइप सिकाउनुका साथै अन्य सबै
टाइप सम्बन्धि सम्पूर्ण सेवाहरू, टाइप मर्मत गरिन्छ ।

Nobody's perfct.

LOCATION: ISTANBUL TURKEY   CREDIT: PHIL SCOTT

Maybe they're sorry they're stuck here selling tribal art to tourists. By the way, what is "new" tribal art?

LOCATION: PISAC, PERU   CREDIT: JOHN MUMAW

They could have been more specific about what kind of beast it is. Hairy beast? Wild beast?

LOCATION: MIAMI, FLORIDA, USA   CREDIT: LARRY BISHINS

Tax relief.

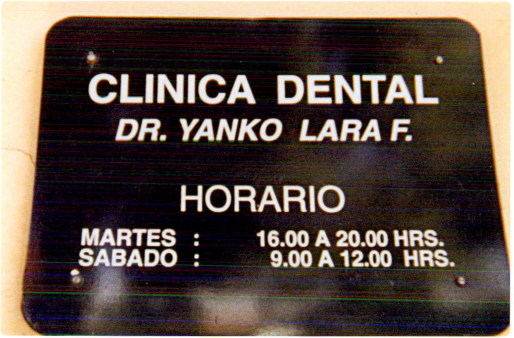

**CLINICA DENTAL**
*DR. YANKO LARA F.*

HORARIO

MARTES  :          16.00 A 20.00 HRS.
SABADO  :          9.00 A 12.00 HRS.

Lara was no doubt destined for the dental profession.

18 咕嚕肉
SWEAT & SOUR PORK
$6.50

Without the photo it could easily be mistaken for a laundry service.

There's something over there, but we're not sure what it is.

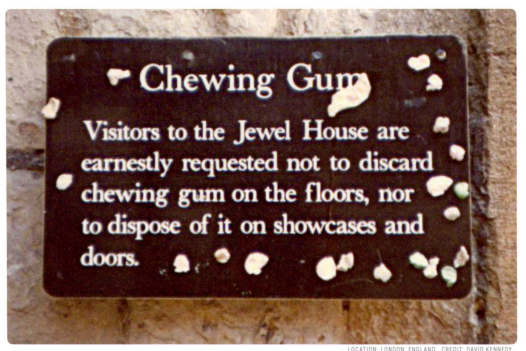

# Chewing Gum

Visitors to the Jewel House are earnestly requested not to discard chewing gum on the floors, nor to dispose of it on showcases and doors.

LOCATION: LONDON, ENGLAND   CREDIT: DAVID KENNEDY

Gum chewers unite. This little "chew in" was staged at the entrance to London's Crown Jewels exhibit.

**Drive-Thru Service**
5 ARBY MELTS
JUST 5$
HURRY IN

LOCATION: PITTSBURGH, PENNSYLVANIA, USA   CREDIT: JEAN BROWN

It looks as though they took the whole "melt" concept a little too far.

Shampoo instructions: wet, wash, rinse, die.

Most minefields forbid entry. It's OK to enter this one as long as you reduce speed.

LOCATION: PINE TOWNSHIP, PENNSYLVANIA, USA   CREDIT: KEN AND TRICIA SUTTON

The emperor's new fence.

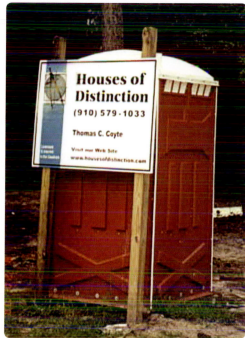

LOCATION: SUNSET BEACH, NORTH CAROLINA, USA   CREDIT: ORWYN SAMPSON

Houses of Distinktion, perhaps? There are some obvious perks: easy mortgage payments, reasonable plumbing bills, and pre-installed air-freshener.

NO MOTORIZED VEHICLES

NO BIKES

NO CAMPING

CAUTION HEAVY TRAFFIC

LOCATION: COLORADO, USA  CREDIT: JOHN B LIBOKY

Are the authorities referring to the weight of the hikers or deer migration in the area?

LOCATION: MARIENVILLE, PENNSYLVANIA, USA   CREDIT: DAVID COBB

Unlimited Happy Meals, eternal french fries, and not a word about cholesterol. What more could the dearly departed want?

# THE LIGHTER SIDE OF DEATH

Some of us might laugh in the face of death, but it's rare that we laugh at death. Death and dying are honored around the planet with a vast range of ceremonies. Even speaking about our mortality can be delicate business. After all, you may be addressing someone who has just suffered a personal loss. And I certainly don't intend to belittle such loss here.

With some distance from the subject, though, it's possible to see that death is no more immune to innuendo than any other topic. And when the sanctity of death is inadvertently trodden upon, it's hard not to crack a smile.

Describing why we may laugh at a sign for the Ronald McDonald Funeral Home (previous page) could almost be the subject of a doctoral thesis. What exactly is it that's funny? Is it that the name evokes the prospect of a heaven filled with unlimited burgers and eternal french fries without the worry of cholesterol? Is it the incongruous contrast: the vision of Happy Meals and a yellow-and-red clown on the one hand, and of coffins and the grim reaper on the other? It's probably better if we just keep it simple: as long as the edges of your mouth curl up, the analysis is irrelevant.

Have you ever wondered what you'd get if you combined a funeral parlor and a flea market?

Your fifteen minutes starts right now.

To stand up after feeding fish, please use your arms to help raise yourself to your knees before placing your weight on your feet one at a time.

Left lane for mid-life crisis; right lane for abandoning New Year's resolutions.

FIRST BAPTIST CHURCH

SUNDAY SERVICES
WORSHIP  10:00AM

NO MAN IS HAPPY
UNLESS HE BELIEVES
HE IS
REV JOHN RITTER PASTOR

LOCATION: AMBRIDGE, PENNSYLVANIA, USA   CREDIT: DAN SADLER

This is one content cleric.

Whaddya know, it is possible to send something straight to hell. The postage must be a killer.

DO NOT FEED THE ELEPHANTS, IT CREATES MANAGEMENT PROBLEMS

Executives battle over elephant feeding.

1998 COW: limited lactose edition. White and brown, high mileage, four stomachs, updated vet shots, makes delicious cereal milk. Winter and summer hooves included.

LOCATION: ROAD TO EUREKA SPRINGS, ARKANSAS, USA   CREDIT: KENNETH KUJAWA

Nothing captures the spirit of Easter like a little handgun action.
Reserve your firearm now for next Easter so you don't miss out on the fun.

ARGUE & PHIBBS

SEAN McTERNAN B.A.

EAMON MacGOWAN B.A.

SOLICITORS

LOCATION: COUNTY MAYO, IRELAND   CREDIT: PETE WILLIAMSON

Finally, a little competition for Dooey, Cheatum & Howe.*

*In America, it's commonly written as Dewey, Cheatum & Howe (with financial services provided by Ima Cheapskate), but in Australasia and Britain "Dewey" is read as "Dyooey" so our crack translation team changed it for the sake of greater global understanding and humor appreciation.

LOCATION: DENMARK  CREDIT: DOUG LANSKY

At least they're telling it as it is! But the "+" makes it look like some sort of equation: bad plus toilet equals…hold it until you get home.

LOCATION: MAZATLAN, MEXICO  CREDIT: JOYCE KURTH

"Please press one if your child is drowning, press two if it's your spouse, press three if you don't know the victim. Or hold for a lifeguard."

LOCATION: SAN LUIS OBISPO, CALIFORNIA, USA  CREDIT: LARRY KAVANAUGH

It's nice to see that cutting-edge technology is helping to take the confusion out of sign reading.

LOCATION: MAUI, HAWAII, USA  CREDIT: SCOTT MASON

OK, nearly bottomless.

# SAY WHAT?

Established languages constantly evolve and new ones are created. For instance, Hinglish, a street-savvy combination of Hindi and English, is now spoken by some 350 million Indians but wasn't in mainstream use just ten years ago. Even though millions of Indians speak English, companies have had to catch on to this new linguistic trend in a hurry. Domino's Pizza, for example, changed their "Are you hungry?" campaign to "Hungry kya?" McDonald's even came up with a slogan that mirrors Hinglish's unorthodox construction: "What your bahana is?" ("Bahana" means "excuse," so this is intended to translate as "What's your excuse for eating at McDonald's not home?")

All languages present challenges. There are times when you see a sign so bungled you wonder if you've just read the work of a translator who's about to get the sack. But there's one minor problem with that theory: you're in a country where English is the primary language.

We've all caught typos in books and magazines that have squeaked past the editorial gatekeepers. When a flagrant English error is flapping about in a public space for all to see, you think someone will point it out. And yet it's not easy to bring the error to the attention of those responsible. There's never a "comment box" attached to a sign or billboard. There's no obvious person to call, and no public-syntax bureau – or if there is, it doesn't post its telephone number.

They don't call it a safety ladder for nothing. Or, on second thought, perhaps they do.

If you see rain or snow, take shelter immediately.

中西结合

癌痛治疗中心

PAINFUL TREATMENT CENTER OF CANCER

Imagine the fine print: "Other cancer centers may claim results, but we have some of the most painful treatment available. Just wait until you try some of our exciting services. We can help take your pain to a new level. And if you have cancer but don't have any pain yet, we can help with that too."

If you're going to live in a place named Cape Fear, you need a positive outlook on life.
Here at the Optimist Club, people see the cape half full.

Just kidding, go ahead and walk in front of traffic.

LOCATION: ARIZONA, USA  CREDIT: ANN RICHARDS

Perhaps it's part of a helpful driving-tip series: "sit up" and "keep breathing" signs are up ahead.

Hey, I hooked a feisty one.

LOCATION: INCLINE VILLAGE, NEVADA, USA   CREDIT: NORMAN ROSENBERG

The new college-admissions scheme.

LOCATION: WAIANAPANAPA STATE PARK, MAUI, HAWAII, USA   CREDIT: JOHN GRIFFEN

They're still excavating lost luggage.

Your vehicle will rise up and get an oil change. All traffic violations will be forgiven.

**Some Kind of Fish from The Red Sea**

This photo was taken in the Alexandria Aquarium, or as the employees there like to call it: "Some kind of place that keeps fish in tanks."

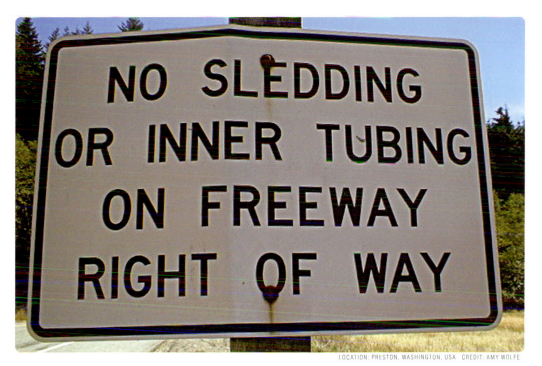

NO SLEDDING OR INNER TUBING ON FREEWAY RIGHT OF WAY

Freeway sledding is now forbidden.

LOCATION: DAHAB, EGYPT  CREDIT: OLGA RETAMOSA

It seems the Prozac arrived before the construction workers had a chance to get started.

Locals are anxiously awaiting the new "Permanent Sign." This temporary one just doesn't fill the void.

LOCATION: ACCRA, GHANA  CREDIT: MATEJ HAJDINJAK

What a good name for a barbershop – it takes some of the pressure off the barber. "Hey, if the Lord wanted you to have straight bangs today He would have held my hand steady."

This may be the smallest recorded ratio of on-site promotional sign to actual attraction.

Responsible parenting.

212
Boring
Oregon City

Maybe the tourist bureau is using reverse psychology.

TOURIST INFORMATION
ONE STOP TRAVEL MART
DON'T PANIC

Now that should put tourists at ease.

TWISTED
PASSION OF CHRIST
DIRTY DANCING

FRESH Hot Dogs    $2.50

LOCATION: FOX THEATRE, WATSONVILLE, CALIFORNIA, USA   CREDIT: ELIZABETH IVANOVICH

Christ is back for an exciting sequel. This time less blood, more salsa.

SHRIMP
TUNA
HIRING
WAITRESS

Wanted: waitress. Must be a strong swimmer and comfortable around bottom feeders. Aquarium experience not required. Please inquire within.

Pssst, it's a secret.

POR HIGIENE NO SE PERMITE INGERIR ALIMENTOS
DENTRO DE LA ALBERCA

DOS HAMBURGUESAS POR PERSONA SOLAMENTE

BECAUSE OF HIGIENIC REASONS IS PROHIBITED TO
EAT INSIDE THE SWIMMING POOL

TWO HAMBURGERS PER PERSON ONLY

From the management: "We're really going to have to insist that you don't bring more than two burgers with you into the water. I'm sure you understand – it's a hygiene issue. Thanks."

LOCATION: TOKYO, JAPAN   CREDIT: THOMAS BURFORD

We have flesh cuts of meat, flesh pasta, flesh vegetables; only the very fleshest food.

LOCATION: WASHINGTON, USA   CREDIT: DOLORES

I don't suppose there's a good word in the English language for a pet area without pets, so both signs were clearly required.

LOCATION: DAYTONA BEACH, FLORIDA, USA   CREDIT: JULIAN BELSH

Attention gators: please write your name, date of birth, and any health conditions. Photo required (partially submerged "log" pose is acceptable).

LOCATION: SUPERIOR, COLORADO, USA   CREDIT: JOHN WAREHAM

Here's a nice rinkside service.

# REJECTED SIGNS

Despite the statement on www.signspotting.com that we don't accept signs made with the intention of being funny, people like sending them in. I've opted not to use these as it could encourage people to start making them, sticking them up in their driveway, and snapping a picture. Plus, funny signs are so much more amusing when the humor is accidental.

Intentionally funny signs come in just a few popular flavors: "Eat here and get gas"; "If you enter this field, you must be able to cross it in nine seconds because the bull can cross it in ten"; "Population: 350 citizens and one old grouchy man"; "Thou shalt not park here"; "Free beer tomorrow"; and "Dogs: please keep owners on leash." Severe warnings such as "Trespassers will be shot, survivors will be shot twice" and site-specific warnings such as "Veterinary hospital parking only: all others will be neutered" are also popular. It's common to use a black marker to add a flying saucer to animal road-crossing signs and to turn speed-bump signs into dead people or animals.

Is this a new Olympic event? Yes, and the guidelines are strict: one reverse is allowed to center the vehicle; use manual transmission only; and there's random urine testing to check for banned substances.

ST. JAMES-BOND UNITED CHURCH
1066 AVENUE RD., TORONTO

Licensed to pray.

R&R WORM FARM

REAR

WORM CASTINGS
&
BEST DIRT
IN TOWN

*Wine Making Supplies Sold Here*

No, actually it's not a French chardonnay.
I made the wine myself with some stuff I bought over at that worm farm.

# BEWARE

## WILD ANIMALS /

## CHILDREN

LOCATION: ISLE OF ERISKA, SCOTLAND   CREDIT: ANNE BUCKINGHAM

Keep your hands away from the cages. You may be clawed, bitten or covered in drool.

Sleeping trees: the flora and fauna will be open for business again at sunrise.

We can't just welcome extraterrestrials; we have to ensure they don't become another ugly traffic statistic.

CAUTION

Please be aware that the balcony is not on ground level.

Caution: hotel management thinks you're stupid.

I'll take the wash, hot wax, and enchilada combo.

You can't say they didn't warn you.

You are now entering mianus.

Drive-by surgery.

Evidently the lemonade stand wasn't working out.

This fried chicken comes in three delicious flavors: regular, unleaded and crispy diesel.

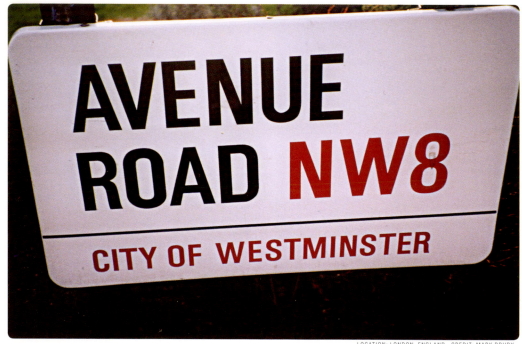

This is an example of early British humor that still stands today.

SITKA VOLUNTEER FIRE DEPT.

GONE     FISHIN
GOOD LUCK !

FIRE CALLS 122     EMS CALLS 371

There's nothing like an emergency-services staff with a sense of humor.

NOTICE

THIS BRIDGE IS RATED FOR A MAXIMUM OF 11 TONS ELEPHANTS ARE THEREFORE REQUESTED TO CROSS TWO AT A TIME ONLY

Elephants take note.

This is how the town of Windpassing (town motto: Grandpa did it) wishes drivers farewell – with what appears to be a rather-difficult-to-enforce local ordinance.

Translating is clearly prohibited at the Karlstejn Castle. Or, as the sign says in Czech just above the English, "Translating Prohibited."

USED RAINBOWS $250 & UP

After you pick one out, swing by my place. I've got some swampland in Mozambique to sell.

Chew, rinse, and spit.

It looks like those clever canines will have to confine their play to dog-friendly courses.

COMPLAINTS
ABOUT ELEPHANTS
TO BE MADE HERE
TOURIST OFFICE, AMBER Ph.530264

LOCATION: JAIPUR, INDIA   CREDIT: NANCY ADOLPHSON

Tusks too long? Ears flopping about? Not taking corners so well?
We understand your elephant problems and we're here to help.

Beware hazardous noises…

Brand new antiques!

You decide: is this sign giving instructions on how to get on an uncomfortable chairlift or is it a promotion for a ski-in/ski-out medical clinic?

Tastier than caged children.

# ACKNOWLEDGEMENTS

This book would not have been possible without the submissions of alert signspotters around the planet; some collected images on the road in far-flung locales, others spotted funny signs blocks from their own homes. Thanks to you, others are able to share the laugh you had when you snapped the picture.

This book took a multiyear detour through Lonely Planet's publishing labyrinth before it picked up a cover, binding, and — something every author anxiously awaits — its own bar code. Commissioning editor Laetitia Clapton put this project on her back and nearly made it to the goal line before handing it over to fellow editor Bridget Blair. Both deserve much credit and thanks for their hard work. Others at Lonely Planet, both past and present, who helped this book along are: Tony Wheeler (an avid sign collector himself, with two entries in this book), Roz Hopkins, and Mariah Bear. A special thanks to Tom Hall at www.lonelyplanet.com, and to all the kind public-relations, marketing and sales people who live and breathe Lonely Planet, whether they're traveling or not.

As a non-native html speaker I was reliant upon Carl Namyst and Richard Warfvinge, who both helped immensely with www.signspotting.com. Markus Ruediger, Steve Roth, Lorne Riley, and Christian Klick at the Star Alliance were kind enough to cough up several round-the-world tickets for grand prizes over the years. And thanks to my agent, Michael Bourret, who has likely been skimming down this page – he always skims, he never reads – and wondering why he hasn't seen his name earlier. (That's because I save the best for last.)

OK, having said that, I now feel compelled to add one more person (sorry Michael). My wife deserves a double serving of thanks for helping open signspotting submissions when my hands were tired, looking over my pithy captions – often chiming in with excellent suggestions of her own – and keeping the photos out of the hands of our three-year-old, Sienna, who badly wanted to touch and play with the photos for the utterly understandable reason that this was forbidden.

**Signspotting: Absurd and Amusing
Signs from Around the World**
October 2005
ISBN 1 74104 489 8

Published by
Lonely Planet Publications Pty Ltd
ABN 36 005 607 983
© Doug Lansky 2005
© photographers as indicated 2005
Cover photograph by
Lonely Planet Images: Outback road in
Western Australia, Greg Elms

Printed through
Toppan Security Printing Pte. Ltd.
Printed in Singapore

Publisher: Chris Rennie
Senior Commissioning Editor:
Laetitia Clapton
Commissioning Editor: Bridget Blair
Design: James Hardy
Layout: Indra Kilfoyle
Editors: Kate Evans and Sarah Bailey

**LONELY PLANET OFFICES**
**Australia**
Head Office
Locked Bag 1, Footscray, Victoria 3011
☎ 03 8379 8000, fax 03 8379 8111
talk2us@lonelyplanet.com.au

**USA**
150 Linden St, Oakland, CA 94607
☎ 510 250 6400
fax 510 893 8572, info@lonelyplanet.com

**UK**
2nd floor, 186 City Rd,
London EC1V 2NT
☎ 020 7106 2100, fax 020 7106 2101
go@lonelyplanet.co.uk